East Anglian Steam Gallery (PART FIVE)

INTRODUCTION

C000205829

One glance at an East Anglian railway map any time until the early sixties would re
criss-crossing mainly flat and at times rather desolate terrain. The fact that many starting p
virtually in the middle of nowhere was bound to focus attention from cost-conscious mana
Beeching hit the headlines.

Notable complete closures were the Mid-Suffolk (1952) and the M&GN (1959). Many line
services after passenger trains had ceased to run, prime examples being Bentley–Hadleigl
Market–Framlingham (1952), freight (1965); Mellis–Eye (1931), freight (1964); Bishop's S
(1966); and Thaxted–Elsenham (1952), freight (1953). The rot had begun to set in, and East Anglia by virtue of its wide open
spaces, competitive road transport, and a dramatic increase in private cars could not sustain its network of branch lines. The
mid-sixties saw many hundreds of track miles removed forever.

Alternatively main lines from Liverpool Street enjoyed prosperity and handled a highly efficient integrated commuter system
(the last word in surburban steam operation), seasonal traffic to the various coastal resorts, Continental boat trains and during
1951/2 some of the fastest trains in Britain.

With the theme of contrasts firmly in mind East Anglian Steam Gallery Part Five takes another pictorial tour of the Eastern
Counties, starting in the Ipswich area—illustrating the diverse nature of locomotives and train services during the fifties and early
sixties.

John D. Mann, Frinton-on-Sea, 1990

ACKNOWLEDGEMENTS

East Anglian Steam Gallery – Part Five could not have materialised without the support and enthusiasm of contributors to the
series, many of whom have willingly loaned priceless negatives or supplied prints. Sincere thanks go to: P. J. Kelly, A. R. J. Frost,
A.I.I.P., A.R.P.S., M.I.R.T., Dr W. J. Naunton, J. Brodribb, P. J. Snell (Essex Bus Enthusiasts' Group, F. Church Collection),
P. H. Groom, F. Hornby, P. J. Lynch, my colleague Win Cole and the dedicated staff of the Lavenham Press Ltd. Special thanks
are extended to J. P. Wilson for the selection of superb vinatge M&GN scenes. I am also indebted to my friend Malcolm Root
G.R.A. for pointing out that after extensive studies of Reedham Junction in connection with a painting, the print of a Class K3
(East Anglian Steam Gallery – Part Four – page 25), is in fact reversed. Additionally, Class E4 No 62794 at Colchester (North) in
the same volume (page 34), is about to leave 'for' Cambridge.—Apologies to all concerned.

FRONT COVER
BENTLEY JUNCTION – January 4th 1959. A striking view of Class B1
No 61270 clearing Belstead Bank south of Ipswich, with the 'up' 08.24
Sundays only Peterborough to Colchester train.   (*Photo* – A. R. J. Frost)

INSIDE FRONT COVER
IPSWICH – May 12th 1915. A wartime view of the G.E.R. goods yard
(No. 1 Road). The train is a consignment of G.S. wagons headed by a class
J66 (L.N.E.R. Classification) tank.
    (*Photo* – Ransomes Reading Collection, courtesy A. R. J. Frost)

BACK COVER
LIVERPOOL STREET – 1959. Britannia Pacific No 70039 "SIR CHRISTOPHER
WREN" and Class L1 No 67702 bask in the sunshine awaiting departure.
    (*Photo* – A. R. J. Frost)

THIS PAGE
NEAR THURSTON – April 19th 1952. Class B12/3 No 61570 on an Ipswich–
Cambridge train, passes No 61577 on a Bury St Edmunds–Ipswich working.
    (*Photo* – P. J. Lynch)

Copyright and design, South Anglia Productions.
Published by South Anglia Productions, 26 Rainham Way, Frinton-on-Sea, Essex CO13 9NS
ISBN 1 871277 04 3
Printed in England by The Lavenham Press Ltd.

IPSWICH DOCKS. March 25th 1954. When trolley buses rejened supreme... note the overhead wires. Class J70 No 68025 is shunting wagons. Also

IPSWICH (Wherstead Road) – 1958. With cab tarpaulin in position an unidentified Class J15 leaves the docks with a short freight. The hoardings and road vehicles (Kommer Karrier lorry and Ford Thames van) are worthy of mention.

(*Photo* – J. Brodribb collection)

IPSWICH (Stoke tunnel) – 1949. A magnificent photograph of great detail. An unidentified Class L1 is about to enter the tunnel from the Colchester end. The assembled stock, P.W. hut and tool box possibly from an Ex-G.E. tender are extremely interesting.

IPSWICH – May 5th 1951. A local train sets out behind Class D16/2 No 62590 in her last year of service. The posters (left of picture) are represen-
tative of the period.

(Photo – P. J. Kelley)

IPSWICH – 1958. The "unique" Class K5 No 61863 (rebuilt from K3 in 1945) and the only example to enter service, waits to depart on a down train.

IPSWICH – November 27th 1954. The impressive Goods Junction box gantry no longer graces the Ipswich skyline; on a dismal day Class B12/3 No 61569 arrives with the 1.30pm from Bury St Edmunds.

(*Photo* – P. J. Kelley)

BURY ST EDMUNDS – May 25th 1953. Superb station architecture provides a backdrop for Class E4 No 62783 leaving with the 1.50pm train to Long Melford. Behind the tender is a Gresley J15 f... one ...

BURY ST EDMUNDS – October 30th 1954. Locomotives "on shed" are Class J17s Nos 65580/89, and Class J15 No 65420 built Stratford 1892 fitted with spark arrestor chimney.

(*Photo* – P. J. Kelley)

FORDHAM – Mid 1950s. A Cambridge University Railway Club special leaves with Class E4 No. 62785 in charge.   (Photo – Dr. W. J. Newton)

MARCH – April 10th 1960. East Anglia's last steam outpost – in the foreground is Class D16/3 No 62613, the final "Claud" to remain in service.

(Photo – P. J. Kelley)

MARCH – September 20th 1956. Class B17/1 No 61621 "HATFIELD HOUSE" on shed. A Thompson "matchboard" full brake can be observed behind the loco.
(Photo. R. H. Green)

CROMER BEACH – July 15th 1935.
M&GN 4–4–0 No 45 leaves with a train
for Melton Constable.
(*Photo* – J. P. Wilson)

CROMER BEACH – July 19th 1935.
M&GN 4–4–0 No 51 shunting in the
summer sunshine.
(*Photo* – J. P. Wilson)

CROMER BEACH – May 2nd 1939.
Class D3 No 4373 climbs away from
Beach station with a Melton Constable
bound train.   (*Photo* – J. P. Wilson)

CROMER BEACH – July 3rd 1935.
M&GN No 53 in immaculate condition
passes with a Melton Constable train.
(*Photo* – J. P. Wilson)

NEAR CROMER – July 9th 1934.
M&GN 4–4–0 No 1 on a Cromer
Beach–North Walsham train near
Cromer links halt.
(*Photo* – J. P. Wilson)

NEWSTEAD LANE JUNCTION –
July 10th 1934. M&GN 4–4–0 No 2
heads a Cromer Beach–North Walsham
train. (*Photo* – J. P. Wilson)

RUNTON WEST JUNCTION– July 9th 1934. The 3.00pm Cromer Beach–Melton Constable approaches hauled by M&GN No 2.

(*Photo* – J. P. Wilson)

KELLING SIDING – July 8th 1935. Another classic vintage scene. M&GN No 91 is working a Cromer–Melton Constable train.

(*Photo* – J. P. Wilson)

SOUTH LYNN – May 30th 1939. A Spalding–King's Lynn train leaves behind M&GN 4–4–0 No 013. Note the lower quadrant semaphore gantry.

(*Photo* – J. P. Wilson)

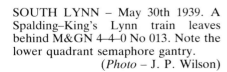

NORWICH (Thorpe) – September 2nd 1951.
Thompson design Class L1 No 67788 passes the site which is now occupied by Crown Point maintenance depot, with a local train from Cromer.

NORWICH (Thorpe) – April 10th 1961. The Norfolk terminus is beautifully captured in this view. Britannia Pacific No 70012 "JOHN OF GAUNT" departs on a Liverpool Street express. A Derby Lightweight D.M.U. and a Brush type 2 (later Class 31) can also be seen.

(*Photo* – P. H. Groom)

NORWICH (Thorpe) – April 10th 1961. Another view on the same day. Class J15 No 65469 is on station pilot duties; in the background Class B1 No 61005 is being turned. Note the L.N.E.R. concrete hut positioned under the signalbox steps.

(Photo – R. H. Groom)

NORWICH (Thorpe) – September 2nd 1951. It is 12.15pm and Class J15 No 65417 is on the turntable minus smokebox number plate. To assist identification the cabside number has been cleaned. A B1 is over the ashpit and a Britannia Pacific can be observed near the coaling cenotaph.

(Photo – P. J. Kelley)

NORWICH (Thorpe) – July 19th 1954. The 4.45pm from Yarmouth Vauxhall runs in behind Class D16/3 No 62586. The train is a mixture of G.E. and L.R. Mk 1 stock with a Stanier coach adjacent to the locomotive.
(Photo – P J Kelley)

NORWICH (Thorpe) – July 19th 1954. Britannia Pacific No 70035 "RUDYARD KIPLING" brings in the down "Broadsman" and passes varied semaphore signalling.

(Photo – P. J. Kelley)

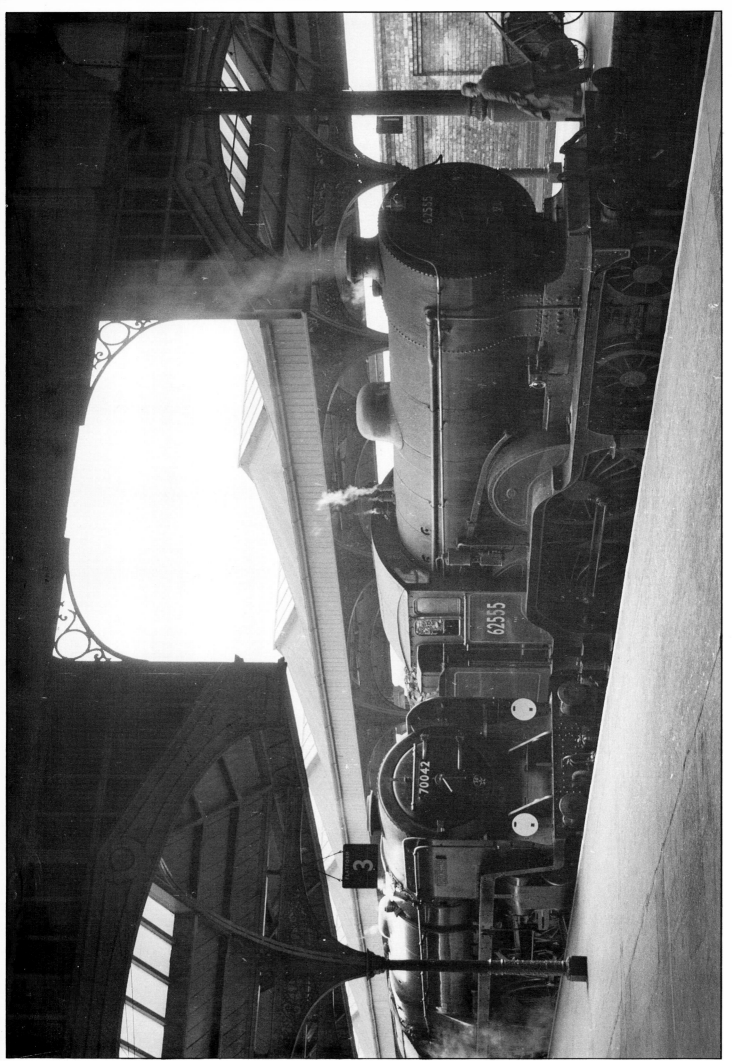

NORWICH (Thorpe) – October 1st 1955. Motive power contrasts are evident in this photograph of Class 7MT No 70042 "LORD ROBERTS", on the 10.30am from Liverpool Street, and Class D16/3 No 62555.

(Photo – P. J. Kelley)

NORWICH (Thorpe) – September 2nd 1951. Class K1 No 62018 waits impatiently with the 2.34pm to Liverpool Street via Cambridge.

(*Photo* – P. J. Kelley)

LOWESTOFT – April 21st 1957. A clean Class F6 No 67231 simmers on shed. The cab detail can be clearly seen along with patchwork repairs to the tank and bunker sheeting.

(Photo – P I Kelley)

LOWESTOFT – Mid 1950s. Class L1 No 67714 leaves with a passenger working on a misty morning.

(*Photo* – Dr. W. J. Naunton)

BECCLES – May 28th 1960. Class J15s No 65469 and 65462 (now preserved) set out with an M&GN Society special. Railtours became very popular during the 1950s and often provided the unexpected, as in this case. 65469 had become a failure and 65462 (later inheriting the former's stovepipe chimney) was sent to assist.

(Photo – Dr. W. J. Naunton)

BECCLES – September 30th 1956. Another railtour. "The Suffolk Venturer", organised by "The Railway Enthusiasts' Club", is double headed by Class E4 No 62797 and Class J15 No 65447, for many years the Mid Suffolk line's regular engine.

(Photo – F. Hornby)

EYE – Mid 1950s. At the terminus of the branch from Mellis (Ipswich–Norwich main line) Class E4 No 62797 is running round a "Norfolk Railway Society" special. On this occasion the loco is immaculately turned out.
(*Photo* – Dr. W. J. Naunton)

HAUGHLEY JUNCTION – July 26th 1952. Class J15 No 65447 is the centre of attention, having just arrived from Laxfield with the last passenger train over the Mid Suffolk Light Railway. (*Photo* – P. J. Kelley)

MARLESFORD – 1958. The "Framlingham Goods" crosses the A12 on a bleak winter's day, with Class J15 No 65389 in charge. Station buildings (right of loco) survive today. The garage and various signs are noteworthy in this fascinating view.

(Photo – J. Brodribb collection)

PARKESTON – July 9th 1955. The down "Day Continental" arrives behind Class B1 No 61233. Note the flat bottomed to Bullhead track connection on the "up" line.

(*Photo* – P. J. Kelley)

PARKESTON QUAY – January 9th 1955. A striking angle on Class J15 No 65453, leaving with a single 15 ton S.R. brake van.

(Photo – P. J. Kelley)

PARKESTON QUAY – July 9th 1955. The up "Scandinavian" gets under way. An Ex-L.N.E.R. six wheel passenger brake van is immediately behind the tender of Class B1 No 61223.

(*Photo* – P. J. Kelley)

COLCHESTER (North) — May 24th 1958. A study of Class B17/4 No 61667 "BRADFORD" having just arrived on the 11.04am train from Cambridge.

(Photo: E. Hornby)

KELVEDON (Low level) – May 5th 1951. Another last train – Class J69/1 No 68578 is about to leave for Tollesbury suitably embellished for the occasion. Note the gentleman smartly dressed in plus four trousers on the platform.

(Photo – P. J. Kelly)

BRAINTREE – September 1958. W.D. No 90480 is engaged in shunting activities. This branch, once part of the through route to Bishop's Stortford, was electrified in 1977.

(Photo – J. Brodribb collection)

BRAINTREE – September 1958. Class F6 No 67227 has just arrived with the branch train from Witham. A Morris Royal Mail van is ready to receive its load. (*Photo* – J. Brodribb collection)

EAST HORNDON – September 6th 1958. After a night of heavy rain, 5th April 1958, single line working is in operation due to severe flooding. 2–6–4T No 42223 is crossing Standard 2–6–4T No 80080, now preserved. Note detonator boxes on both roads near the driving wheels of the Standard tank.

(Photo – E. Church, courtesy Essex Bus Enthusiasts' Group)

NEAR WESTCLIFF-ON-SEA – November 10th 1958. Another highly detailed view. Fairburn 2-6-4T No 42679 is approaching Crowstone Road footbridge on a sunny morning.
(*Photo* – F. Church, courtesy Essex Bus Enthusiasts' Group)

SOUTHEND (Central) – November 9th 1958. Standard tank No 80101 enters the station through autumn mist, passing sister engine No 80077 at the station. F. Church, courtesy Essex Bus Enthusiasts' Group.)

SOUTHEND (Central) – July 5th 1959. A passenger train arrives during bridge alterations in readiness for electrification, hauled by Standard tank No 80097.

(*Photo* – F. Church, courtesy Essex Bus Enthusiasts' Group)

SHOEBURYNESS – Autumn 1951. A general view again showing considerable detail. A pair of unidentified 2–6–4Ts are passing another 2–6–4T

(Photo: E. Church, courtesy Essex Bus Enthusiasts' Group)

TILBURY (Riverside) – July 19th 1959. Class 4F No 43934 into the station. Class 4F No 43935 is drawing the "Orient Line" boat train and train engine No 43934 into the station.
(*Photo* – F. Church, courtesy Essex Bus Enthusiasts' Group)

TILBURY (M.P.D.) – July 18th 1959. Stanier tank No 42528 is shunting S.R. Class Q1 No 33018 and M.R. 3F No 47512.

PLAISTOW – December 20th 1958. Ex-LTS engines awaiting scrapping – 4-4-2T No 41950, 0-6-2Ts (Whitelegg) Nos 41990–41992, 41985–41984–41993, and 4-4-2Ts Nos 41977–41978–41958.
(*Photo –* F. Church, courtesy Essex Bus Enthusiasts' Group)

FENCHURCH STREET – September 15th 1958. Fairburn tank No 42678 brings in empty stock, while Standard tank No 80133 waits on the loco

PALACE GATES – October 23rd 1948. Class G5 No 7322, one of three from the N.E., allocated to the G.E. section, on a Seven Sisters train. They were later transferred to Saffron Walden (sub shed of Cambridge) for working between Audley End and Bartlow. (*Photo* – P. J. Lynch)

LIVERPOOL STREET – 1959. A study of Class B1 No 61300 at the London terminus. Note the track keys have been renewed in the foreground;